RAPID STUDY SKILLS FOR STUDENTS:
IMPROVING YOUR MEMORY
POCKETBOOK

www.How2Become.com

Orders: Please contact How2Become Ltd, Suite 1, 60 Churchill Square Business Centre, Kings Hill, Kent ME19 4YU.

You can order through Amazon.co.uk under ISBN 9781912370122, via the website www.How-2Become.com, Gardners or Bertrams.

ISBN: 9781912370122

First published in 2018 by How2Become Ltd.

Typeset for How2Become Ltd by Gemma Butler.
Printed and bound by CPI Group (UK Ltd, Croydon, CR0 4YY

Disclaimer

Every effort has been made to ensure that the information contained within this guide is accurate at the time of publication. How2Become Ltd is not responsible for anyone failing any part of any selection process as a result of the information contained within this guide. How2Become Ltd and their authors cannot accept any responsibility for any errors or omissions within this guide, however caused. No responsibility for loss or damage occasioned by any person acting, or refraining from action, as a result of the material in this publication can be accepted by How2Become Ltd.

The information within this guide does not represent the views of any third-party service or organisation.

Contents

INTRODUCTION

Hello, and welcome to your new pocketbook, *Improving Your Memory*. Through the course of this guide, we will talk you through what memory is, and how you can train yourself to improve your memory skills to benefit your studies, as well as your everyday life!

So, we're going to start by taking a look at 'how memory works' in a basic sense, including how your body stores memories, and what neuroscientists believe about how the brain works to allow us to retain and recall what we experience every day.

Next, we'll move on to the lifestyle changes that you can make in order to give your memory a boost! Then, we'll talk you through some specific techniques you can employ during your studies to increase how well you can remember things.

Finally, you can put these new skills to the test by playing our selection of memory games. Practising these will sharpen your skills to no end!

HOW DOES MEMORY WORK?

Our first step is to take a look at how memory works. With this in mind, we'll then move onto ways of improving your memory. Afterwards, you'll have the opportunity to play some sample memory games, which can be used to see how strong your memory is.

SO HOW DOES IT WORK?

While neuroscientists haven't uncovered all of the mysteries regarding the brain, the mind, and consciousness, we have a good understanding of how memories are formed and stored in the brain. In this chapter, we'll be taking a look at the physical elements of memory, such as which processes create memories as well as where memories are held. Then, we'll be moving onto helpful ways about thinking of memory and how it works – ways that will hopefully give you a better understanding of where you need to improve in your revision.

MEMORY – IT'S ALL IN YOUR HEAD

While there are still mysteries about memory, neuroscientists have a good idea about how it works. To start with, long-term memories seem to be stored in the hippocampus, a part of the brain. Memories are formed when neurons in the brain make connections with each other – connections that are never broken. There are millions of neurons in your brain, and each will make many connections to other neurons. This means that you'll be able to retain potentially billions of memories during your lifetime. So, you don't really need to worry about running

out of space. As far as we can currently tell, short-term memories don't involve any physical changes in the brain – this only occurs when a long-term memory is created.

The reason why it's important to know about how the brain itself deals with memories is that it allows you to find out what lifestyle changes allow for you to improve your memory. In particular, some studies suggest that different foods and activities can stimulate the hippocampus and potentially even strengthen connections made between neurons. While this might not mean that eating certain foods will guarantee a better memory, it might be worth looking into.

USEFUL WAYS TO THINK ABOUT MEMORY

While learning about how the brain works is fascinating and useful in some ways, it isn't entirely helpful just to think of your memory as a billion neurons making connections. Thankfully, some psychologists have specialised in creating models of memory that attempt to describe how it feels for us to create and store memories.

While there's some dispute over which model is the most accurate, these models can still make the concept of memory much easier to understand.

You might have noticed that, in this book, we've referred to 'short-term' and 'long-term' memory. This is a popular way of thinking about memory, but it isn't entirely accepted across the board by psychologists. Some researchers disagree on whether short-term and long-term memory are two distinct systems in the brain, but instead are a single unit. Whatever the case, it appears that the brain can temporarily hold some memory, and also store it for longer periods of time while also being able to manipulate it to some degree.

So, short-term memory seems to be the place where memories are first stored upon creation. Some people refer to this as 'working memory' since it's the information that you're using in the current moment. There isn't a complete consensus on how much the short-term memory can hold and for how long, but studies show that information in your short-term memory tends to last between 15 and 30 seconds. This is fine when you need to remember a phone number for a few seconds, or remember which cupboard your food goes in, but it isn't particularly useful for remembering large portions of information to recall in an exam.

For studying, you really want to make use of your long-term memory. Long-term memory is different for a number of reasons. Firstly, the creation of long-term memories involves physical changes in the brain. When a long-term memory is formed, more connections are made between the neurons inside your brain. In addition, long-term memory is held permanently, whilst short-term memories can only be held for a limited amount of time. Even if you can't remember it anymore, it's likely that the memories are still in your brain somewhere – you're just having difficulty recalling them.

It might be helpful to think of the long-term memory as a massive hard drive, filled with all kinds of information. Life events, facts, as well as instructions on how to perform certain actions, are all stored in here. As time progresses, you'll gather more memories, meaning that your brain ends up storing a lot of information. Naturally, some memories will be used less than others, and these ones tend to be harder to recall. Essentially, the more you use a memory, the easier it will be to recall.

This might be why most revision techniques encourage you to repeat phrases, or recall them on the spot (e.g. flashcards). When revising, bear this in mind – make sure you're recalling all the information you've learned, so that it will be easier to do so in the exam. It also seems that you're more likely to remember something if you're in an environment that you originally learned it in, or had an experience in. For example, if you first experienced driving in a certain city, you'll likely be reminded of it when you revisit that same place. This means that sitting practice papers in a controlled environment might be useful for remembering things, since sitting in the exam room might jog your memory.

HOW CAN I IMPROVE MY MEMORY?

Your brain can store huge amounts of information, so you don't need to worry about expanding the capacity of your brain. The brain has approximately a billion neurons in it, and each of these can form over one thousand connections to other neurons. This means that there are over a trillion connections in the human brain. If each of these connections accounts for a single memory, then that means your brain can store one trillion memories.

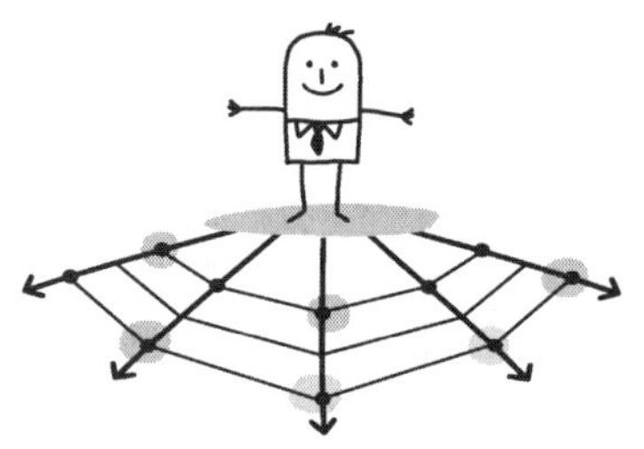

If this is true, you don't need to worry about your brain running out of storage space.

Instead, people who want to improve their memory need to focus on the following:

- Making sure information is committed to long-term memory;

- Finding reliable ways to recall these memories easily.

We'll be taking a look at both of these in more detail, looking at tricks which you can use to improve in both areas.

SENDING INFORMATION TO LONG-TERM MEMORY

As we've discussed, information starts by existing in the short-term memory. This is where memories you need in the moment are kept, and can only last reliably for up to 30 seconds. After this, they either disappear entirely or become inaccurate.

For this reason, you need to make sure the information you're absorbing in your revision enters the long-term memory. Lots of things get stored in your long-term memory without much conscious effort on your part, but this doesn't mean you can read a page once and expect it all to be absorbed.

You need to focus on the information and use techniques to create strong connections. A lot of people find that associating information with certain things can be useful. Rewriting information in your own words, or discussing it in your own words with a friend, is usually a good way of committing information to long-term memory. You'll associate facts with where you are and who you're talking to, and rewording the information will prove that you understand it.

There are a few other methods, all with some scientific evidence, which allow you to strengthen memories and commit them more easily. Scientists have found a connection between chewing gum while studying and committing more memories to long-term memory, potentially because chewing gum stimulates the hippocampus (the part of the brain which handles memory). Other studies suggest that drinking coffee helps consolidation of information to long-term memory.

However, remember that a dependence on caffeine can put you at a disadvantage when you're in the exam room. Finally, some studies suggest that eating berries can improve your ability to commit information to the long-term memory. This might be worth trying if you want to gain an extra advantage when it comes to studying.

IMPROVING RECOLLECTION

Once you've committed things to long-term memory, you need to work on recollection techniques. As previously mentioned, memories that get used often end up being easier to recall. For example, you can probably remember things like your telephone number, home address, or internet passwords easily because you write, say, or type them a lot. Think about your passwords that are saved automatically. When you eventually have to type them in again, are they more difficult to remember? If this is the case for you, then it's because you haven't had to recall it as much.

So, one of the best ways to improve recollection is to test yourself regularly. Almost every revision tactic does this, but the ones that are best suited for this are flashcards, reciting key facts out loud, learning games, and mind maps. Try and do these without looking at your notes so that you can test how strong your ability to recall is.

There are a few other methods which also help to improve recall, including some lifestyle changes. Some studies show that both meditation and exercise can help to strengthen your recall ability. In addition, getting a good night's sleep regularly has been linked to stronger memory. Try these for yourself and see how they work for you.

On top of memories being easier to recall if they're used often, some studies show that creating strong associations between things can make memories easier to recall. For a moment, think of your brain as an attic or large storage locker, and all of the objects inside it represent memories. The ones closest to the entrance are the ones you take out and put back in most regularly, so they're the easiest to recall. However, what about the belongings at the back? Getting to those, or even being able to see them in the darkness, can prove to be incredibly difficult. Now imagine tying a piece of rope to each of these objects, and leaving the loose end near the entrance of the locker. You could follow each of these to find the

objects at the back of the room. These pieces of rope represent associations made in your mind, so that these memories are easier to recall.

In the next chapter, we're going to take a look at some of the methods you can use to create these associations, as well as the day-to-day steps you can take to boost your memory.

TECHNIQUES TO BOOST YOUR MEMORY

A good place to start when working to improve your memory is your everyday routine. By this, we mean that adjusting your lifestyle choices in several little ways can improve memory retention and recollection.

While the following tips seem simple, it cannot be understated just how important they are if you want to see fast improvement in your mental sharpness!

1. Cementing sleep 

Of course, getting enough sleep is an essential part of maintaining both your physical and mental health. Therefore, nailing down a good 8 hours goes hand-in-hand with having a good memory! Not only this, though, but memories become cemented in our minds during an undisturbed sleep, making REM sleep incredibly important for the retention of the day's events in the brain.

2. Exercise those cells

One of the most important reasons to exercise is for the boost in brain function. Physical exertion helps to maintain the health of brain cells, and even serves to stimulate the development of new blood vessels in the brain. This all serves to increase how much information you can store in your brain, as well as how quickly you can recall it.

3. Water work

Drinking enough water is a very easy act of self-care to neglect, but one that has a widespread impact should you do so. Dehydration is disastrous for cognitive function – studies have shown that even being slightly dehydrated can restrict how much information we are able to take in and process. The NHS recommends that to be at peak performance, you should drink around 1.5 to 2 litres of water per day. Of course, alcohol consumption is tied to memory loss, and for good reason. Cutting down can reduce nitrates in your brain, which are tied to unhappy brains!

4. Brain food

Similarly, there are certain foods that you should look at if you want to improve your memory, as well as some that you should avoid! You won't be too surprised by what you see here! Leafy vegetables and fruit are ones that are known to aid cognitive function, while wholegrains are believed to aid concentration, which in turn will help how well you can retain and recall information. Foods like white bread and processed meat bring toxins into the body, which can impair efficient brain function.

5. Destress yourself

Taking steps to reduce your general stress levels will benefit you on your quest to improve your memory, for one simple reason. When you are feeling stressed, it is because your brain has triggered the production of 'stress hormones'. While this is happening, some other brain functions are suppressed, including the formation of lucid memories. In other words, when you're stressed, your brain does not prioritise solidifying your experiences of the day as memories in your head! So, don't be so hard on yourself, take time to unwind every day.

Now the basics are out of the way, let's go onto the specific techniques you can employ when aiming to memorise any amount of content you need to know.

CREATE REPRESENTATIONS IN YOUR BRAIN

This method of making associations is most common, and can be applied to almost any kind of information with a bit of ingenuity. Essentially, you want to give your own meaning to facts and data by representing them in a unique way. For example, if you needed to remember that the Easter Rising in Ireland occurred in 1916, you could imagine a pile of Easter eggs going up in an elevator to floor 1916. This might seem bizarre, but these types of association can help you remember important details more easily. If you're any good at drawing, it might even help to make brief sketches for the most important things you need to know!

CHUNKING

Chunking is the process of chopping up larger pieces of information into smaller pieces, so that you can remember them more easily. This is particularly useful for things like phone numbers, but can also be used for academic study too. For example, say that you need to memorise a mathematical formula or method for solving a certain kind of maths problem. You could dissect the whole solution into smaller steps, then memorise the process. Then, you can apply the above method for creating representations for each step, or use the method of loci (explained below).

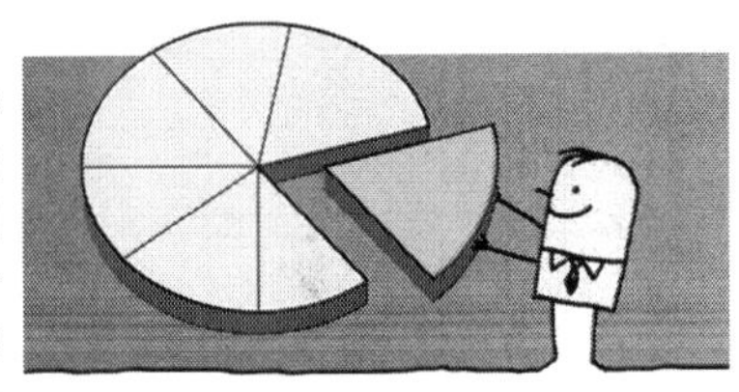

METHOD OF LOCI

This is a technique that dates all the way back to the ancient Greeks and Romans, and involves mentally visualising locations and attaching information to them.

First, think of a familiar place, such as your bedroom, classroom, or office. Alternatively, you can imagine a route that you take regularly, like your commute to work or school. Then, start to imagine placing the information you need to remember in this environment, such as key dates or names. Once you've done this, try to keep the location in your mind. This means that, when you think of this location, you'll also be able to recall the memories that you've 'placed' there.

CONCLUSION

In this chapter, we've taken a look at how memory works, as well as ways to improve your memory. In particular, candidates who want to make sure that their memory is at its peak should focus on improving their recollection, since this is what you'll have to rely on under timed conditions in an exam.

Make use of the tips above and apply them to the revision methods that we've outlined in our chapter on learning styles. This way, you'll make sure that you're committing as much information as possible to your long-term memory, and creating ways to recall it quickly.

In the next chapter, you'll have the opportunity to try out some memory games for yourself, so you can see how strong your working memory is, as well as test your long-term memory and recollection.

MEMORY GAME 1 – REMEMBERING WORDS IN ORDER

All of the methods in the previous chapter are great for strengthening your long-term memory and recollection, but now you have the opportunity to attempt some memory games. These are a great way to test your memory, as well as have a bit of fun.

SAMPLE MEMORY GAME 1: REMEMBERING WORDS IN ORDER

In this game, you'll need to remember the order of different words. In the first variation of the game, you'll just need to memorise the order, since you'll be given the list of words at the very end. In later exercises, you'll need to recall the words as well as their order, making things a little more difficult. Try not to look at each exercise for any longer than 30 seconds for the easier questions, and no longer than a minute for the tougher, later questions.

Exercise 1

Memorise the words in the following list:

1	Shotgun
2	Giant
3	Coyote
4	Jade
5	Ghost

Now, rearrange the words listed here so they're in the same order as on the previous page:

Giant	Coyote	Jade	Shotgun	Ghost

1	
2	
3	
4	
5	

Exercise 2

Memorise the words in the following list:

1	Crab
2	Axis
3	Crypt
4	Pancakes
5	Apple
6	Garage
7	Salt
8	Jewel
9	Ladybird
10	Glove

Now, rearrange the words listed here so they're in the same order as on the previous page:

Pancakes	Crypt	Glove	Salt	Apple
Ladybird	Crab	Axis	Garage	Jewel

1	
2	
3	
4	
5	
6	
7	
8	
9	
10	

Exercise 3

Memorise the words in the following list:

1	Virtual
2	Night
3	Ghoul
4	Power
5	Gadget
6	Dart
7	Jar
8	Injustice
9	Horizon
10	Cyclops

Now, rearrange the words listed here so they're in the same order as on the previous page:

Jar	Injustice	Ghoul	Horizon	Power
Virtual	Dart	Cyclops	Night	Gadget

1	
2	
3	
4	
5	
6	
7	
8	
9	
10	

Exercise 4

Memorise the words in the following list:

1	Dread
2	District
3	Fierce
4	Leaf
5	Milk
6	Poet
7	Prong
8	Lock
9	Blip
10	Echo

Now, rearrange the words listed here so they're in the same order as on the previous page:

Lock	Dread	Poet	Milk	Leaf
Echo	Blip	District	Prong	Fierce

1	
2	
3	
4	
5	
6	
7	
8	
9	
10	

Exercise 5

Memorise the words in the following list:

1	Wolf
2	Feet
3	Cola
4	Bin
5	Gymnast
6	Hormone
7	Legend
8	Dove
9	Wilderness
10	Joyride

Now, rearrange the words listed here so they're in the same order as on the previous page:

Hormone	Cola	Wilderness	Gymnast	Feet
Wolf	Bin	Joyride	Legend	Dove

1	
2	
3	
4	
5	
6	
7	
8	
9	
10	

Exercise 6

For these questions, you need to memorise the words as well their order:

1	General
2	Cat
3	Bar
4	Care
5	Amphibian

Now, write the words in the order that they appeared on the previous page:

1	
2	
3	
4	
5	

Exercise 7

For these questions, you need to memorise the words as well their order:

1	Brawl
2	Glitter
3	Aroma
4	Cottage
5	Captain
6	Cinder
7	Twin
8	Bull
9	Cellblock
10	Gateway

Now, write the words in the order that they appeared on the previous page:

1	
2	
3	
4	
5	
6	
7	
8	
9	
10	

Exercise 8

For these questions, you need to memorise the words as well their order:

1	Steel
2	Seed
3	Crush
4	Uprising
5	Jump
6	Barbarian
7	Pavement
8	Elimination
9	Faint
10	Bear

Now, write the words in the order that they appeared on the previous page:

1	
2	
3	
4	
5	
6	
7	
8	
9	
10	

Exercise 9

For these questions, you need to memorise the words as well their order:

1	Plastic
2	Boutique
3	Harmonica
4	Firstborn
5	Beam
6	Archaeology
7	Drive
8	Swamp
9	Angle
10	Lemon

Now, write the words in the order that they appeared on the previous page:

1	
2	
3	
4	
5	
6	
7	
8	
9	
10	

Exercise 10

For these questions, you need to memorise the words as well their order:

1	Nightfall
2	Wax
3	Skull
4	Annual
5	Goggles
6	Diamond
7	Faith
8	Scar
9	Pill
10	Ceremony

Now, write the words in the order that they appeared on the previous page:

1	
2	
3	
4	
5	
6	
7	
8	
9	
10	

MEMORY GAME 2 – WORD RECOLLECTION

SAMPLE MEMORY GAME 2: WORD RECOLLECTION GAME

For this game, we're going to give you a list of words. Each of these words has been assigned to a number. Your goal in this exercise is to remember both the words and the numbers given to each. Look at the list for a short period of time (no more than 30 seconds for the shorter lists, and no more than a minute for the longer ones), turn the page over and write the words which correspond to each number.

Exercise 1

1	Fang
2	Dirt
3	Cloud
4	Phantom
5	Hook

Now, without looking at the above list, write the words which correspond to each number:

1	
3	
4	
2	
5	

Exercise 2

1	Empire
2	Injury
3	Evil
4	Air
5	Doctor

Now, without looking at the above list, write the words which correspond to each number:

4	
1	
3	
2	
5	

Exercise 3

1	Sword
2	Guest
3	Lottery
4	Savage
5	Bacteria
6	Fist
7	Frost
8	Hamster
9	Rib
10	Airport

Now, without looking at the above list, write the words which correspond to each number:

6	
10	
3	
8	
4	
2	
5	
7	
9	
1	

Exercise 4

1	Alien
2	Gorilla
3	Metal
4	Chief
5	Ankle
6	Barricade
7	Coincidence
8	Badger
9	Escalator
10	Detox

Now, without looking at the above list, write the words which correspond to each number:

10	
8	
2	
1	
3	
5	
7	
6	
9	
4	

Exercise 5

1	Panda
2	Jewel
3	Fuzz
4	Grin
5	Convict
6	Bite
7	Hippopotamus
8	Firm
9	Public
10	Column
11	Hero
12	Fringe
13	Courage
14	Arrow
15	Icicle

Now, without looking at the above list, write the words which correspond to each number:

3	
10	
5	
1	
9	
15	
12	
14	
8	
6	

11	
2	
7	
4	
13	

Exercise 6

1	Chance
2	Town
3	Big
4	Bust
5	Dough
6	Night
7	Skyline
8	Chicken
9	Behaviour
10	Boat

Now, without looking at the above list, write the words which correspond to each number:

4	
5	
1	
2	
8	
10	
3	
7	
6	
9	

Exercise 7

1	Goat
2	Aqua
3	Purple
4	Strap
5	Klaxton
6	Tear
7	Balloon
8	Note
9	Tapestry
10	Collect

Now, without looking at the above list, write the words which correspond to each number:

10	
2	
4	
8	
7	
3	
5	
6	
9	
1	

Exercise 8

1	Throw
2	Hoop
3	Shoe
4	Dunk
5	Travel
6	Shorts
7	Hook
8	Chest
9	Pass
10	Bench

Now, without looking at the above list, write the words which correspond to each number:

2	
7	
3	
5	
8	
4	
9	
6	
10	
1	

Exercise 9

1	Indicate
2	Spell
3	Attest
4	Banquet
5	Sea
6	Vindicate
7	Arrest
8	Blank
9	Acorn
10	Bat

Now, without looking at the above list, write the words which correspond to each number:

5	
10	
2	
6	
4	
9	
8	
7	
1	
3	

Exercise 10

1	Troll
2	Milk
3	Squawk
4	Day
5	Karate
6	System
7	Bird
8	Authority
9	Electric
10	Dance

Now, without looking at the above list, write the words which correspond to each number:

6	
2	
9	
3	
7	
5	
10	
8	
1	
4	

Once you're done, head over to the answer section to see how well you did.

MEMORY GAME 3 – LONG-TERM MEMORY

FREEFORM MEMORY GAME – LONG-TERM MEMORY

In this section, you have the opportunity to test your long-term memory with information that you need to know. For this section, write down 10 key facts or details that you need to know for your own exam. Then, go away for a few days, and use some revision techniques to remember these key facts. In a week's time, come back to these facts and see how well you remember them.

Fact Number	Fact
1	
2	
3	
4	

5	
6	
7	
8	
9	
10	

MEMORY GAMES – ANSWERS

REMEMBERING WORDS IN ORDER

Exercise 1

1	Shotgun
2	Giant
3	Coyote
4	Jade
5	Ghost

Exercise 2

1	Crab
2	Axis
3	Crypt
4	Pancakes
5	Apple
6	Garage
7	Salt
8	Jewel
9	Ladybird
10	Glove

Exercise 3

1	Virtual
2	Night
3	Ghoul
4	Power
5	Gadget
6	Dart
7	Jar
8	Injustice
9	Horizon
10	Cyclops

Exercise 4

1	Dread
2	District
3	Fierce
4	Leaf
5	Milk
6	Poet
7	Prong
8	Lock
9	Blip
10	Echo

Exercise 5

1	Wolf
2	Feet
3	Cola
4	Bin
5	Gymnast
6	Hormone
7	Legend
8	Dove
9	Wilderness
10	Joyride

Exercise 6

1	General
2	Cat
3	Bar
4	Care
5	Amphibian

Exercise 7

1	Brawl
2	Glitter
3	Aroma
4	Cottage
5	Captain
6	Cinder

7	Twin
8	Bull
9	Cellblock
10	Gateway

Exercise 8

1	Steel
2	Seed
3	Crush
4	Uprising
5	Jump
6	Barbarian
7	Pavement
8	Elimination
9	Faint
10	Bear

Exercise 9

1	Plastic
2	Boutique
3	Harmonica
4	Firstborn
5	Beam
6	Archaeology
7	Drive
8	Swamp
9	Angle
10	Lemon

Exercise 10

1	Nightfall
2	Wax
3	Skull
4	Annual
5	Goggles
6	Diamond
7	Faith
8	Scar
9	Pill
10	Ceremony

WORD RECOLLECTION GAME

Exercise 1

1	Fang
3	Cloud
4	Phantom
2	Dirt
5	Hook

Exercise 2

4	Air
1	Empire
3	Evil
2	Injury
5	Doctor

Exercise 3

6	Fist
10	Airport
3	Lottery
8	Hamster
4	Savage
2	Guest
5	Bacteria
7	Frost
9	Rib
1	Sword

Exercise 4

10	Detox
8	Badger
2	Gorilla
1	Alien
3	Metal
5	Ankle
7	Coincidence
6	Barricade
9	Escalator
4	Chief

Exercise 5

3	Fuzz
10	Column
5	Convict
1	Panda
9	Public
15	Icicle
12	Fringe
14	Arrow
8	Firm
6	Bite
11	Hero
2	Jewel
7	Hippopotamus
4	Grin
13	Courage

Exercise 6

4	Bust
5	Dough
1	Chance
2	Town
8	Chicken
10	Boat
3	Big
7	Skyline
6	Night
9	Behaviour

Exercise 7

10	Collect
2	Aqua
4	Strap
8	Note
7	Balloon
3	Purple
5	Klaxton
6	Tear
9	Tapestry
1	Goat

Exercise 8

2	Hoop
7	Hook
3	Shoe
5	Travel
8	Chest
4	Dunk
9	Pass
6	Shorts
10	Bench
1	Throw

Exercise 9

5	Sea
10	Bat
2	Spell
6	Vindicate
4	Banquet
9	Acorn
8	Blank
7	Arrest
1	Indicate
3	Attest

Exercise 10

6	System
2	Milk
9	Electric
3	Squawk
7	Bird
5	Karate
10	Dance
8	Authority
1	Troll
4	Day

CONCLUSION

So, you now should have a much better understanding about how your memory works, and what you can do to improve it, both in a general sense as well as specific actions you can take. You can use this book as a base to find out even more about how to make use of your memory, and how to improve it to make your revision as effective as possible.

A FEW FINAL WORDS...

You have reached the end of your guide. If you have read the information in this book and made use of the tips provided, you should be on your way to improving your memory, which will go a long way to helping you pass your exams comfortably and making yourself proud. Hopefully, you will feel far more confident in what you know as well as what you need to improve.

For any test, it is helpful to consider the following...

The Three 'P's

Preparation. Preparation is key to passing any test; you won't be doing yourself any favours by not taking the time to prepare. Many fail their tests because they did not know what to expect or did not know what their own weaknesses were. Take the time to re-read any areas you may have struggled with. By doing this, you will become familiar with how you will perform on the day of the test.

Perseverance. If you set your sights on a goal and stick to it, you are more likely to succeed. Obstacles and setbacks are common when trying to achieve something great, and you shouldn't shy away from them. Instead, face the tougher parts of the test, even if you feel defeated. If you need to, take a break from your work to relax and then return with renewed vigour. If you fail the test, take the time to consider why you failed, gather your strength and try again.

Performance. How well you perform will be the result of your preparation and perseverance. Remember to relax when taking the test and try not to panic. Believe in your own abilities, practise as much as you can, and motivate yourself constantly. Nothing is gained without hard work and determination, and this applies to how you perform on the day of the test.

Good luck with your exams. We wish you the best of luck in all of your future endeavours!

USEFUL RESOURCES

	MON	TUE	WED	THUR	FRI	SAT	SUN
09:00 - 10:00							
10:00 - 11:00							
11:00 - 12:00							
12:00 - 13:00							
13:00 - 14:00							
14:00 - 15:00							

	MON	TUE	WED	THUR	FRI	SAT	SUN
15:00 - 16:00							
16:00 - 17:00							
17:00 - 18:00							
18:00 - 19:00							
19:00 - 20:00							
20:00 - 21:00							

	MON	TUE	WED	THUR	FRI	SAT	SUN
09:00 - 10:00							
10:00 - 11:00							
11:00 - 12:00							
12:00 - 13:00							
13:00 - 14:00							
14:00 - 15:00							

	MON	TUE	WED	THUR	FRI	SAT	SUN
15:00 - 16:00							
16:00 - 17:00							
17:00 - 18:00							
18:00 - 19:00							
19:00 - 20:00							
20:00 - 21:00							

	MON	TUE	WED	THUR	FRI	SAT	SUN
09:00 - 10:00							
10:00 - 11:00							
11:00 - 12:00							
12:00 - 13:00							
13:00 - 14:00							
14:00 - 15:00							

	MON	TUE	WED	THUR	FRI	SAT	SUN
15:00 - 16:00							
16:00 - 17:00							
17:00 - 18:00							
18:00 - 19:00							
19:00 - 20:00							
20:00 - 21:00							

	MON	TUE	WED	THUR	FRI	SAT	SUN
09:00 - 10:00							
10:00 - 11:00							
11:00 - 12:00							
12:00 - 13:00							
13:00 - 14:00							
14:00 - 15:00							

	MON	TUE	WED	THUR	FRI	SAT	SUN
15:00 - 16:00							
16:00 - 17:00							
17:00 - 18:00							
18:00 - 19:00							
19:00 - 20:00							
20:00 - 21:00							

WANT TO LEARN EVEN MORE REVISION TRICKS?

CHECK OUT OUR OTHER REVISION GUIDES:

Achieve 100% Series

FOR MORE INFORMATION ON OUR REVISION GUIDES, PLEASE CHECK OUT THE FOLLOWING:

WWW.HOW2BECOME.COM

Rapid Study Skills for Students Series

Get Access To

FREE Psychometric Tests

www.PsychometricTestsOnline.co.uk

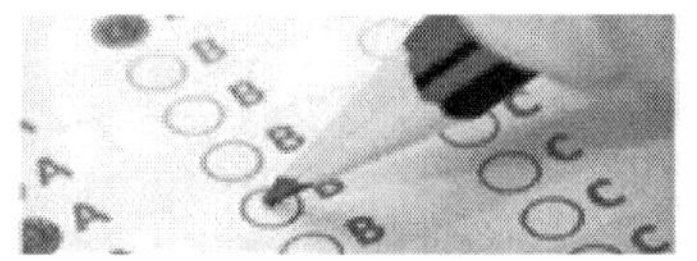

Printed and bound by CPI Group (UK) Ltd, Croydon, CR0 4YY

06/07/2026

02157570-0003